Bill Woodrow

FOOLS' GOLD

Bill Woodrow

FOOLS' GOLD

Tate Publishing

**Sponsored by
Romulus
Construction
Limited**

ISBN 1 85437 199 1

Published by order of the Trustees 1996
for the exhibition at the Tate Gallery
23 January 1996 – 28 April 1996 and at the
Institut Mathildenhöhe, Darmstadt
20 October 1996 – 5 January 1997

Published by Tate Publishing,
Millbank, London SW1P 4RG
© Tate Gallery 1996 All rights reserved
Designed and typeset by Caroline Johnston
Printed and bound in Great Britain
by Balding and Mansell, Peterborough

Front cover
**Anchor (Dredged from the First
Wreck of the 'Ship of Fools')** 1995, p.37

Back cover
In Awe of the Pawnbroker 1994
(detail), pp.48–9
Photo: John Kellet

Photographic Acknowledgments
All photographs © the artist except:
John Kellet, p.28, back cover
National Gallery of Canada, Ottawa, p.17 (below)
Sue Ormerod, London, p.26
© Werner Zellien, Berlin, p.43
Edward Woodman, p.16
Jerry Young, pp.33, 51

Contents

Sponsor's Foreword

Romulus Construction Limited is sponsoring this exhibition of new and recent works by Bill Woodrow. Romulus have previously sponsored exhibitions of work by Phillip King at Fulham Broadway, Barry Flanagan at The Whitechapel and David Nash at The Serpentine Gallery.

Foreword

Bill Woodrow, one of the generation of British sculptors who came to prominence in the early 1980s, is an artist of wit and invention whose art is informed by what he encounters in daily life. Until the late 1980s he made sculptures from found, defunct consumer objects, cutting out forms to release distinctive images infused with a deep sense of irony. They were reminders of loss and waste in an epoch of high consumerism as well as an affirmative statement that, phoenix-like, out of the discarded object could arise a new one. Although these early works were often visual puns, Woodrow increasingly engaged with issues related to ecology, nuclear power and matters of a broadly sociological nature. His interest in such themes has continued to the present day.

In 1987 Woodrow ceased his activity of metal cutting and in 1989 took up bronze casting. The sculptures in this exhibition are bronzes made since 1990 and are all connected with the theme of personal and global survival. Woodrow has built a vocabulary of forms which express a deep sense of foreboding tinged with irony. Pawnbrokers' signs, mutated animals, gold coins, blasted trees, padlocks and chains present a bleak picture of an anarchic world rushing headlong towards self destruction. Woodrow's sculptures raise questions about many of today's important issues.

This is the first exhibition of Woodrow's sculpture to take place in a public gallery in this country since 1989, and we are pleased too that it will subsequently be shown in the Institut Mathildenhöhe, Darmstadt. We are delighted that the artist has accepted our invitation to make a show in our series of sculpture exhibitions held in the Duveen Galleries, now in its fifth year. We are grateful to N. & S. Mosse of Kilfane Falls for lending to the exhibition and to Sculpture at Goodwood for releasing a sculpture on loan to them from the artist. We would also like to thank John Roberts for the stimulating essay he has contributed to this publication, which looks at Woodrow's work within the context of the legacy of Marcel Duchamp. We are delighted to acknowledge the support of Romulus Construction Limited and are very grateful to Douglas Woolf for his personal interest in the project. However, our deepest debt is to Bill Woodrow for the enthusiasm and commitment he has shown in bringing this project to fruition.

Nicholas Serota
Director, Tate Gallery

The Sculpture of Bill Woodrow: Casting between the Currents

John Roberts

I have a vivid image of Bill Woodrow, or at least the Bill Woodrow I first got to know. It is the early morning and the streets of Brixton and Peckham are deserted, save for the slow progress of council refuse collectors. Driving a hired transit van Woodrow navigates his way around the back streets from Railton Road up to Acre Lane. He is in first gear, not slow enough to be suspicious, not fast enough to miss what might be lying unnoticed on the pavement or on waste ground. He stops; he can see the edge of a television poking out of a skip full of old carpets and broken furniture. Quickly, efficiently, the television is removed and carefully strapped in the back of the van. This has been a good haul; three televisions, one washing machine, two umbrellas and a filing cabinet.

Part extrapolation from the real conditions of his practice, and part wish-fulfilment on my part, this is of course a description of Woodrow as urban 'rag-picker' and scavenger that verges on the deliciously mythic. Alone on the streets, 'thieving' in the name of art, Woodrow's resource-shopping takes on an illicit, proletarian edge: Woodrow as the surreptitious gleaner. It also summons up an image of the contemporary artist as archaeologist and preservationist; moving amongst what has become discarded, remain-dered and without discernable value, Woodrow attests to the critical power of art to release the 'secret' contents of everyday objects. To reclaim and to re-present is at the same time a discursive act of bringing forth.

The notion of the artist as 'rag-picker' is a compelling identity that has not only shaped Woodrow's art, but has dominated so much art since the late 1970s that has looked back to the strategies of the early avant-garde. However, the days of street scavenging are long over for Woodrow, or at least for the foreseeable future. Since the late 1980s Woodrow has closed down the indomitable and popular image of himself as an appropriationist. In 1986 he began to produce huge, welded constructions. Seemingly precar-ious and monstrous at the same time, a number of these works appeared to mimic what the earlier work had been determined to leave behind: mod-ernist sculpture's articulation of interdependent forms. Furthermore, from 1989 Woodrow began to cast in bronze, firstly small figures and objects, then large complex arrangements of figures, animals and everyday objects as his confidence in the medium grew. For anyone only familiar with the early work these are extraordinary moves that seem openly to confront the critical ideals of the early sculpture. To turn from a found-object based aesthetic to bronze casting might appear to confound, even demote, the dominant appropriationist ethos of our period. Yet, for all the appearance of distance from the early work, the found-object based sculpture still under-writes the new work. It furnishes it with its vocabulary of symbols and, despite certain inflexions to the contrary, an anti-modernist commitment to the artist as narrator. In this respect Woodrow's aesthetic reflexes as a sculptor have always been those of an image-maker. The judgements he has made about the social function of sculpture have been determined by a commitment to the strong, iconic, story-telling image. This is why there is more than a formal coincidence between 'Camera and Lizard' (1981) and 'Source Pot' (1991). Yet this is not to establish a false continuity for the sake of aesthetic and biographical convenience. Rather it is to reveal – contrary to the majority of critical literature on Woodrow's early sculpture – that the radical change in procedures is not a return to 'traditional skills', but the elaboration and presentation of another set of skills. Despite its deconstructive mode, the early sculpture is in fact the work of someone highly skilled in cutting metal, plastic and leather and in improvised fabrication. There is certainly an ironic tension, therefore, in the replacement of the physical manipulation of found objects by bronze casting. That which initially appears to be indifferent to traditional forms of sculptural procedure demonstrates an abundance of 'craftsmanship'; just as what appears to be the result of lengthy technical adjustment and manual labour is actually the product of the labour of others at the foundry. This tension, I argue, is not a pleasant conceit, but fundamental to the problems and contradictions that Woodrow had to address if he was to continue to produce work with a

left
Camera and Lizard 1981
Camera
16 × 27 × 13cm
BW46

right
Source Pot I 1991
Bronze, glass and man's jacket
76 × 107 × 102cm
Private Collection
BW350

degree of openness. I would contend, then, that the move to bronze casting is not anything so simple as a break with an earlier 'radical self-image', but actually a re-complication of the long problematic relationship between skill, value and meaning in twentieth-century art. If the early cut-out pieces placed the skills of the sculptor in quotation marks, the current bronzes do something similar, moving the bounds of authorship into an industrial and reproducible process. There is a sense therefore that the move into bronze casting is in itself 'quotational', a second-order – if highly elaborate – re-employment of traditional skills.

Just as by the late 1970s the Minimalist ethos had made it difficult to produce images in sculpture, since the late 1980s and the academic acceptance of appropriation in art, the reworking of traditional skills has presented the opportunity to break with what had become dominant practice. The ideological framework in which 'skill' is posed and positioned is here very different from those interminable debates on proper artistic skills that underscored the backlash against late Modernism and Conceptual art in the early 1980s, particularly in Britain. Woodrow is not a curmudgeonly defender of traditional skills as the lost ground of artistic value and authenticity. For Woodrow the use of traditional skills is determined by their appropriateness, something that enables a certain job to be completed, a certain set of effects to be followed through. As such, the issue of artists 'risking' something new, in order to restate their autonomy, needs to be placed against the wider sense of artists adjusting their procedures to contingent issues and problems.

Both pre-modern and modern sculpture are predicated on a simple set of formal and textual distinctions: concealment/revelation, disguise/disclosure, inside/outside, exterior/interior. In fact, in making any three-dimensional object the artist is concerned with exploring the tension between presentation (display, showing forth) and the promise of interiority (what lies beyond immediate vision). However, since Marcel Duchamp at the beginning of the twentieth century, the logic and demands of presentation have dominated the theory and practice of sculpture. Duchamp's reduction of art-making to the presentation of found objects or 'ready-mades' contributed to the radical transformation of the categories of sculpture (although Duchamp had no specific interest in the condition of modern sculpture, he was not producing *anti*-sculpture).

The incorporation of the found object into the institutional spaces of art – museums and galleries – made the reliance on older, craft-based forms of art-making increasingly unstable. Putting aside Duchamp's own taste for the provocative, therefore, what this move initiated was the convergence of the 'making' of the artwork with the demonstration and execution of the artist's conceptual judgement or critical perception. This is more than the simple – and simple-minded – assertion that art is what artists say is art. Rather, it is a vindication that the skill in art is not necessarily identifiable with the crafting of objects supposedly derived from the expression of the artists' 'innermost feelings'. Thus Duchamp's commitment to presentation can be read as a radical attack on the presumed links between manual dexterity, expressiveness and value. The effects of this have been enormous and manifold. For in contributing to the release of the found-object into the experience of art, Duchamp's move prefigured the two major concerns of avant-garde and modern art this century: the production of an art of the everyday which incorporated rather than simply represented everyday objects, and the production of an art that was not reliant on the traditional categories of painting and sculpture. In these terms Duchamp's practice has been described as a variant of montage. This is certainly true. Like photo-montage the presentation of a found object in a gallery is a disruptive, decontextualising act. But the implications of Duchamp's move discloses something more profound: that is, what is repeated is not the same. The meaning of the urinal in the store Duchamp bought it from is not the same as the meaning of the urinal in the gallery, just as the meaning of the same urinal is transformed once its representation is incorporated into another work of art. Duchamp suggests that the separation of manual artistic skills from value releases the meaning of the object from being determined by its location within traditional aesthetic categories. The found object, therefore, is able to assert its autonomy as a sign, facilitating the institutional break-down between definitions of the aesthetic and non-aesthetic.

The influence on post-1960s neo-avant-garde art of this attack on the tra-ditionally regarded separation between art and the categories of the every-day is incontestable. From Minimalism and 'process art' to Post-minimalism and the cult of industrial fabrication, the display of unmediated materials has been associated with a certain 'realism'. For instance the 1969 show at the Whitney Museum of American Art in New York, *Anti-Illusion: Procedures/Materials*, which included Carl Andre, Michael Asher, Eva Hesse, Bruce Nauman and Richard Serra, defended the display of material process in terms of a commitment to the 'real' and actual. Although this period of work had little or no interest in the signifying content of found objects, the presence of Duchamp's legacy is nonetheless indisputable. Minimalism and its aftermath celebrated factual presentation or 'literalness' as the laying bare of all artistic pretensions to expressive interiority. In fact the notion of interiority is almost mocked in many of the works of the period. Robert

Untitled 1979
Plaster
17 × 120 × 110cm
BW1

Morris's steel cubes only allow the viewer the most tantalising and frustrating glimpse of what might lie beyond their polished surfaces.

This commitment to presentation and the reordering of definitions of artistic skill haunts Bill Woodrow's work. The influence of Minimalism and Post-minimalism is clearly evident in the early sculptures. In the 'geological' and proto-found-object pieces of the late 1970s, Woodrow consciously identifies the meaning of the work with the visible evidence of its making. In the case of the 'geological' sculpture this involves the casting and embedding of everyday objects in concrete (for instance the hair-dryers in 'Untitled' (1979)), or covering actual everyday objects themselves in concrete (as for example a vacuum cleaner in 'The Long Aspirator', (1979)), which are then partially revealed by chipping away at parts of the surface. As with Minimalism, what is demonstrated here is the sense that the experience of modern sculpture is an evidential one, that its commitment to the 'real' stands or falls by how it expresses a resistance to the aestheticisation and the symbolisation of the artist's feelings. But for Woodrow there is additionally something larger at stake than a post-aesthetic commitment to the display of material process as evidence of the 'real'. For what characterises these early moves is an emergent identification with what Minimalism had suppressed in its reading of the Duchampian legacy: the allegorical presentation of the object, the fact that in becoming something else in the gallery or

The Long Aspirator 1979
Vacuum cleaner and concrete
45 × 740 × 45cm
BW 6

museum the found object can establish a narrative connection with the
everyday. Although critical of Modernism's formal concerns, Minimalism
was still critical of the association between imagery and the loss of high
seriousness. For Duchamp though, such 'low' or demotic content was
always central to the transcendental aims of the avant-garde: the bridging of
the higher genres of art with such bodily experiences and pleasures of the
everyday as intoxication, humour and sexual desire. The failure of Minimalism can be seen in its conflation between seriousness and the exclusion of
these non-specialist or 'philistine' forms of spectactorship. Judgements of
truth and value were taken to lie in an implacable denial of the false or
deceptive pleasures of bodily sensuality.

   Like many artists of his generation Woodrow stepped into this breach,
taking on picture-making and the allegorical treatment of the object as a
defiant return to the pleasures of the everyday. What was perceived as being
lost to art for this generation was the artist's and spectator's familiarity with
the object-world that most people living in the industrialised West now
took for granted: namely the late capitalist world of the commodity and its
spectacular modes of publicity and presentation. From the late 1970s
onwards we can see Woodrow finding his way into these new spaces, confi-
dent in the knowledge that the work was participating in a new cultural
agenda. Sculpture could now incorporate everyday objects without fear or

embarrassment of aesthetic triviality (which, it can be argued, had always affected that earlier counter-modernist tradition of sculpture produced under the influence of Pop Art). A key transitional work on this score for Woodrow is 'Hoover Breakdown' (1979) in which he presents the constitutive parts of a Hoover vacuum cleaner next to a wooden replica of the original machine. The replica appears to be sucking up the elements. This work demonstrates two significant things in Woodrow's development. The presentation of a real object without manipulation (that is, without a reliance on its partial disguise) and the presentation of a real object as a deep source of mimetic pleasure and cultural identification. In the spirit of the demotic Duchamp, Woodrow offers up both a 'deconstructed' image of an everyday (if by then outmoded) object and its physical simulation as a way of bridging the gap between the world of sculpture and the world of the everyday object. But at the same time, this is an uncanny, 'deranged' process, in which the presentation of the habitual does not appear as it should; what is supposedly ordinary, banal even, becomes underscored by the images of anxiety, loss and violence. The Hoover's breakdown is also the retching up of the contents of its stomach.

It is these visceral, almost brutal associations involved in the deconstruction or simulation of the found object that provide the leverage for

Hoover Breakdown 1979
Dismantled upright vacuum cleaner with wooden replica painted with black car underseal
96 × 200 × 130cm
BW8

Woodrow's move into the world of the found object *per se*, in such works as 'Twin-Tub with Guitar' (1981). By presenting and manipulating the found object, the object is seen to offer a confirmation of certain shared popular pleasures and a critique of the culture out of which it was produced. The turn to the idea of the found object as a 'host' for the production of other objects was, therefore, more than a charmed discovery; it was the imaginative extension of an allegorical impulse already in place. By producing a 'parasite' object or objects from out of a 'host' object, Woodrow was able to enrich the metonymic and synecdochical content of the found object. The result was the transformation of the use of the found object from its discrete employment to its scenic and narrative reinvention. As such the dialectic between 'host' and 'parasite' produces a vivid elaboration of the tensions between disguise and disclosure, the 'real' and the fabricated in modern sculpture. To look at 'Car Door, Ironing Board and Twin-Tub with North American Indian Headdress' (1981) or 'Life on Earth' (1983) is to see a compelling play-off between presentation of the actual object and illusion, simulation and the 'real', synecdoche and metonymy.

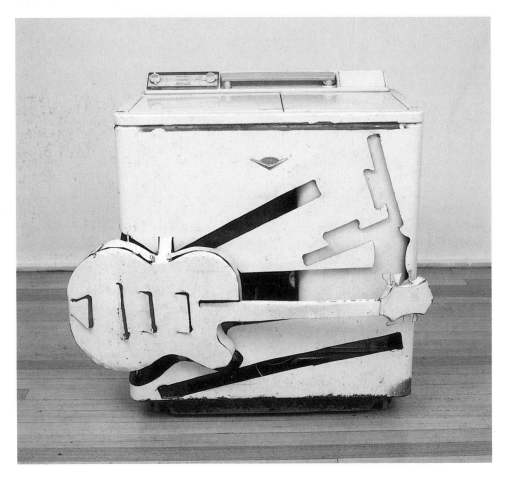

Twin-Tub with Guitar 1981
Washing machine
76 × 89 × 66cm
Tate Gallery
BW 27

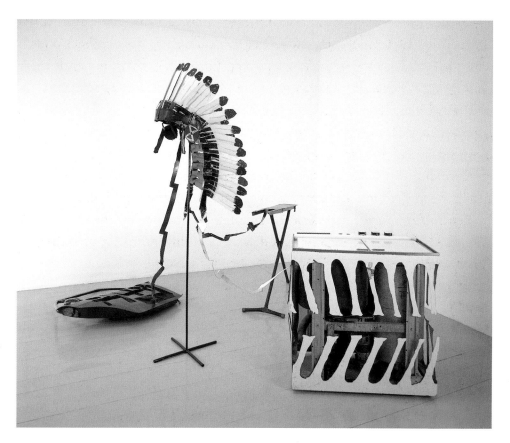

Car Door, Ironing Board and Twin-Tub with North American Indian Headdress 1981
Car door, ironing board, washing machine, enamel paint
Dimensions variable
Tate Gallery
BW50

Life on Earth 1983
Vinyl-covered foam-filled chairs, washing machine
Dimensions variable
National Gallery of Canada, Ottawa
BW114

The point, however, is not that the content of this work is reducible to such oppositions, but that it derives its force from these oppositions. What is so successful about many of these early tableaux is the way in which the making of the work allows different symbolic orders to conflict and fuse with each other. Thus in 'Life on Earth', the representation of the natural world in crisis (in the form of a home-movie screening of a wild-life film) is made from the leather and plastic covers of the chairs on which the comfortable and secure spectators of this crisis are supposedly sitting. What has been transformed industrially from the resources of nature is in turn transformed into materials for a commentary on the limits of the capitalist appropriation of nature's resources. This play between the absence of the natural resource and presence of the resource transformed is a means of staging the contradictions between capitalist demands and the natural world under threat. It is typical of Woodrow's work from this period and of the symbolic choices of much of Woodrow's later work. Nature and culture are in irrevocable and damaging conflict in Woodrow's art. However, there is something specific about the early sculpture within this context that needs to be elaborated on. For what obviously draws Woodrow to a found-object aesthetic during this period is the fact that the found objects he uses – in particular domestic consumer objects – have recently passed from a condition of utility and therefore life, into death (obsolescence). In this respect what gives metaphoric unity to the early and mid-period work is a sense that Woodrow is excavating the forms of a dead culture, a culture locked into the constant replication of the same in the guise of the new. Many other artists in the early 1980s touched on this link between the continuous replacement of the commodity and the loss of a critical consciousness of the past under late modernity, as represented by the media's mythologisation and banalisation of history. In Woodrow, though, this experience of historical loss or bereavement always seemed to be counterpoised by the process of the work's making. While the tableaux were metaphors for the excavation of dead time, they also suggested the transformation of dead labour into a world of new meanings. This may have amounted to an archaeology of the everyday, but it did not stop at the boundaries of the museum; each tableau, small or large, produced a utopian glimpse of the 'world made new' or the 'world turned upside down'. It is no wonder that this work has proved to be so popular, because it seems to speak in epic form of the emancipatory potential held in the dull, repetitive, alienated experiences of everyday life.

In broad terms the early work extends a Post-minimalist concern with process into the realms of 'intellectual montage'. Functional object / art

**Electric Fire, Car Seat and
Incident** 1981
Electric fire and car seat
80 × 300 × 200cm
Southampton City Art Gallery
BW 41

object, presentation/illusion, the real/simulation, the street/the gallery, are
brought into disruptive, unexpected alignment. However, if this owes something to Duchamp's montage-effects, it perhaps owes a greater debt to the
cinema, or rather to cinematic perception. The move into a theatrical space
was at the same time a means of transforming the sculptural notion of the
installation into the filmic notion of the scenic as narrative evidence. Thus
in a number of works from this period, such as 'Car Door, Armchair and
Incident' (1981) and 'Electric Fire, Car Seat and Incident' (1981), the montage
of 'host' and 'parasite' object takes up the filmic techniques of suggestion
and implication to produce a sculptural set-piece, which is equivalent in its
effects to the arrested time of the photograph. The allusion to documentary
practices in the titles and the urban 'dirty realist' content of the images (the
aftermath of violence, the impoverishment and banality of the settings)
reinforces the idea that these works are as much imaginary film-sets as nar-
ratively inflected still-lifes. As an urban 'story-teller' though, Woodrow has
never used the naturalistic human figure (with the exception of the occa-
sional reference to the human head and the inclusion of small, stick-like figures and miniscule babies in the new work). What interests him about the
installation as scenic event or the still-life as allegorical snap-shot is the way

in which human presence and social relations can be inferred, thus allowing the artist to bring into focus the object-world through which humans move. To this end, Woodrow continues that critical scepticism about the naturalistic human figure in sculpture that Minimalism inherited via the early avant-garde, the sense that human depiction invariably confines the work to a humanistic interpretation.

By the late 1980s, therefore, Woodrow had developed a varied set of expressive resources that enabled him to move between different historical and social locations, and between a sense of the art-object as evidence, as narrative and allegorical form. This range was represented in the large number of national and international shows to which he contributed during this period, culminating in his extensive retrospective in Edinburgh in 1986. However, in 1987, what had once appeared rich and compelling became oppressive and overburdened with its own history: in 1987 Woodrow gave up using found objects altogether.

It is always difficult to speculate on why artists make such radical changes: boredom, disappointment, the romance of 'risk-taking' all play their part. But to reduce such change to psychological motives is always to risk substituting the author for the work. This is the familiar mistake of those who consider the intentions of artists as primary. Yet, such changes *are* motivated, which is why the examination of artists' intentions needs to be understood in the context of an analysis of how intentions are permeated by both the internal demands of artistic practices and the pressures of non-artistic forces. Or rather, how these internal demands and pressures interact and diverge to transform the artists' intentions and their and others' representations of such intentions. This is important because the unexpectedness of Woodrow's decision to stop using found objects needs to be treated with complexity and sensitivity.

In turning to welded sculpture in 1987, sculptures which completely abstained from reference to an archaeology of the everyday, Woodrow could almost be said to have rid himself of the burden of what had become too successful: the adroit, even fashionable, notion of himself as the 'man who cuts things out of found objects'. Many artists no doubt dream of such a 'market-profile' which will carry them happily into their old age. Many do not, fearful or apprehensive about what compulsive repetition does to the demands of artistic autonomy. Woodrow, I contend, broke with his immediate past because that past had become routine and academic. The moves that Woodrow could make by cutting one thing out from another were too well known and rehearsed. He was no longer able to learn anything from his working methods, or rather, was rarely surprised by what he learnt from them. Furthermore, the intellectual and cultural terrain upon which such moves had been predicated was also suffering from over-rehearsal.

Woodrow's work emerged into a cultural context in Britain in the early 1980s which was dominated by two things: the debate on Postmodernism and anti-Thatcherite cultural politics. Fundamental to the early debate on Postmodernism was a critique of the 'great divide' between art and popular culture, a divide which late Modernism had done so much to prop up in the name of a certain moral strenuousness. Woodrow's object-pictures, his 'do-it-yourself' sensibility, urban themes and wider sense of crossing disciplinary, aesthetic and cultural boundaries, fitted the bill perfectly. Woodrow was seen as the critical Postmodernist *par excellence*. Moreover, as an archaeologist of the commodity, he was also celebrated as the fertile and mischievous archivist of the new market forces and the effects of capital accumulation. Woodrow was embraced as an astute chronicler of his times. These two formations, though, began to become a burden; it became far too easy to judge and contain the work within this received sociology of culture. In the light of this, Woodrow began to recognise how much the debate on appropriation and bridging the division between art and popular culture had become grossly academic and feeble in itself, particularly now a younger generation of artists took such moves for granted. Quite simply Woodrow wanted out.

As with all artists faced with the critical demands of modern practice, he was forced by a stark choice: either apostasy (the collapse into conservatism) or a rethinking of a critique of the institutional thresholds and boundaries of modern art practice. In other words, either traditionalist affirmation or avant-garde disaffirmation. Woodrow chose the latter, or at least a version of the latter, turning to welded forms to rupture the pattern of his own practice and its increasing cultural status. If this seems merely perverse, it is perversity born of survival, for if a space of renewal is to be opened up by the artist, what is 'out of reach' and 'out of sight' of what passes for dominant artistic practice must be allowed to be tested and evaluated. By taking on a method of making art that his generation had vigorously resisted – welded sculpture – Woodrow adopted the classic avant-garde stance in relation to the problem of artistic autonomy: the pursuit of the illicit, remaindered or out-and-out 'stupid' as a disruption of 'business as usual'. Pertinent and instructive examples of what I mean by this are Francis Picabia's 'monster' paintings of the 1920s. Breaking with the great modernist themes and forms of his early work (the body as machine) Picabia started producing inert, 'scruffy',[1] bad-taste collages full of art jokes and asides. These appeared absolutely incomprehensible to many of his peers:

1 See Dave Beech and Mark Hutchinson, 'Francis Picabia: Another Failure to Interpret the Work', in John Roberts (ed.) *Art Has No History! The Making and Unmaking of Modern Art*, Verso 1994.

nobody could see why he wanted to do them, and nobody wanted to know why. Yet Picabia's 'stupidity' was not so much inane as grievous, a perverse but logical disruption of what he took to be the portentious institutional incorporation of his generation of avant-garde artists into the canon of great art. In effect Picabia had to be 'stupid', to borrow from the illicit, in order to reassert his autonomy. This redefinition of the conditions of autonomy through the illicit and marginal may not work or may not even be recognised as such – as was the case with Picabia – (it may in fact just look stupid), but nevertheless it remains a crucial moment of escape for the artist from the expectations of the moment. The implication of this, of course, is that even if the artists suffers an initial loss or failure by such a move, he or she may stand to gain in the future.

In Woodrow's case, to start producing huge, monstrous Caroesque sculpture was certainly perverse. But it was a perversity that carried before it the argument about what is or is not 'permissible' in contemporary sculpture. For in this move Woodrow was actually able to extend his repertoire of moves. The effect, therefore, was in no sense revivalist but anomalous and awkward. For example in 'The Last Fruit (The Tree of Idleness)' (1988) (a huge fallen tree, crude and schematic, and attached at its perimeters to four open door frames), traditional welded steel sculpture is pushed into an unfamiliar configuration. In early Caroesque Modernism the 'rightness' of the welded joint – its 'good' profile – was considered to be something of inestimable worth. Minimalism mocked this by using steel plates and girders without recourse to 'expressive aesthetics'. Woodrow trumps both positions by using welded steel as a form of picture-making. In this there is an obvious continuity with his early work. But in this case the construction of the image – or scene – is subject to the formal continuities of a single material, even if on occasion Woodrow continues to include actual objects in the work. (In 'The Last Fruit' a television is attached to one of the light stanchions protruding from the doors.) The general effect is of someone now committed to the demands of building things, and therefore thrown back on the need to construct the symbols he requires. In this respect, from 1987 onwards, Woodrow uses the welded object to shift the pursuit of picture-making into what I would call a 'constellational' form of montage. That is, the welded objects (locks and keys become recurring features) form a kind of orrery, as in 'Future Perfect' (1988). The result of this is that Woodrow's major theme – the conflict and interaction of the natural and the cultural – is subject to a different kind of emphasis. Many of Woodrow's early works involve the transformation of the industrial into the natural sign, as if nature was trying to 'escape' from a predatory or dominative appropriation of its resources: the 'host' in this sense is inverted to become the 'parasite'. By contrast, in the welded sculpture, this process of transformation of the industrial into the natural becomes a determining structural feature, to the point in some instances, as in 'The Last Fruit', where they naturally change place. The forces of appropriation appear pervasive. Thus in many pieces made after 1989 the formative and simple idea of one thing changing into another is transfigured into an actual process of mutation. Things become other things; forms grow unexpectedly out of other forms. And this, understandably, is facilitated by the change to welding; welding is essentially a motile and additive process. Hence, what needs to be made clear is that in turning to welding Woodrow was able to re-establish continuity with sculpture as an industrial-based practice (and therefore with modern processes of production) and yet at the same time develop his symbolic resources away from the archaeological.

But if welding appeared perverse in 1987, the move he made in 1989 and 1990 might seem even more so: the use of bronze casting. Unlike welding, in 1989 bronze casting seemed wholly irredeemable[2]. Overwhelmingly associated with aesthetic conservatism and moribund studio practices, bronze was seen not so much as invitingly illicit as lumpen and elitist. Moreover, even to begin to consider casting in bronze the artist would have to be financially secure. Yet Woodrow was not persuaded by such arguments. Bronze casting *was* invitingly illicit, a tradition of sculptural production that was so antithetical to the post-war modern movement and the contemporary ethos of appropriation that it called out to be confronted, transformed and ultimately abused. Woodrow's change to bronze, therefore, can be valued as another way of withdrawing from this prevailing ethos at the same time as offering a critique of the institutional boundaries of sculpture and its intellectual managers. But for Woodrow the initial impetus to change to bronze was not simply a confrontation with the unimaginable. Rather, bronze allowed him to scale down his practice in interestingly unexpected ways: instead of constructing to dominate through scale, the making of small cardboard maquettes for the first bronzes gave him the opportunity to improvise, finesse and model.

In 1989 Woodrow produced a series of bronzes for the Imperial War Museum. These adopted the ideologically shrunken notion of the monumental bronze sculpture to produce an ironic displacement of the category of the memorial. Relatively small in scale and constructed around anti-heroic militaristic details, these works enjoyed disfiguring the high-cultural and sentimental connotations of bronze casting. The war memorial is given another voice: not the voice of paternal authority but of the demotic. It is

2 It needs to be recognised, however, that certain other leading sculptors – for example Tony Cragg, Jeff Koons and Barry Flanagan – were re-engaging with the tradition of bronze casting. But much of this work, I would argue, is revivalist.

easy to misunderstand Woodrow's approach here. Woodrow does not intend to revive some debased notion of modern folk art in the manner of many of those Modernist artists who opted for apostasy. Rather, what concerns him is how in breaking with the prevailing institutional boundaries of sculpture the reworking of would-be illicit forms and genres questions the ideological ownership of those forms and genres. Just as Woodrow turned to welding to expropriate it from its Modernist clients, he turned to bronze to expropriate it from populist and snob alike. This is why this change is a provisional and positional affirmation of bronze casting and not a revival of it. Unlike Michael Sandle in the 1980s, Woodrow is not interested in reclaiming a grand public tradition of bronze sculpture.

There is a two-way subversion that stems from these changes by Woodrow. On the one hand he opens up the Post-minimalist category of sculpture to the crafts of jewellery and the *objet d'art* or table sculpture (everything that has been deemed unworthy of high seriousness in modern art); on the other, he appropriates banal or kitsch objects of domestic or public affection to create an instantly recognisable everyday-object world. It is the former, though, that provides the primary impetus for the move into bronze. The initial down-scaling of his work after the Imperial War Museum series led Woodrow into the production of a large number of small, bronze table-pieces titled 'Little Saints' (1991). As with 'Hoover Breakdown' these are key transitional works, for they transform into new forms and configurations symbols of 'crisis' and 'constraint' introduced after 1987, and adumbrate a range of new symbols (in particular the pawnbroker sign of the three orbs) that eventually formed the basis for larger works. Included in the array of 'Little Saints' are a head of an unidentifiable animal with a ball on its tongue, an alligator emerging from an egg, a pod sprouting four pawnbroker orbs, the bucket of a mechanical digger, one lock connected umbilically to another lock, a playing card emerging from a cup-like body, a nose on top of a pod, a penis or dildo, and a needle and thread with three pawnbroker orbs. These are all attached to a single gold (leaf)-plated ring or halo. The black of the object against the gold of the halo gives the impression that these are charred, petrified objects that have been beknighted or 'spiritualised' in some ironic fashion, objects that have been given a kind of decorative 'after-life'. In fact Woodrow draws on the heat and combustive power of the bronze process itself for his metaphoric effects; many of the pieces appear as if they are in a state of arrested melt-down. This displacement and uglification of the traditional aspirations of the aesthetics of bronze is something that appears intermittently in his work from 1990. What preoccupies Woodrow more, however, is how the look and the asso-

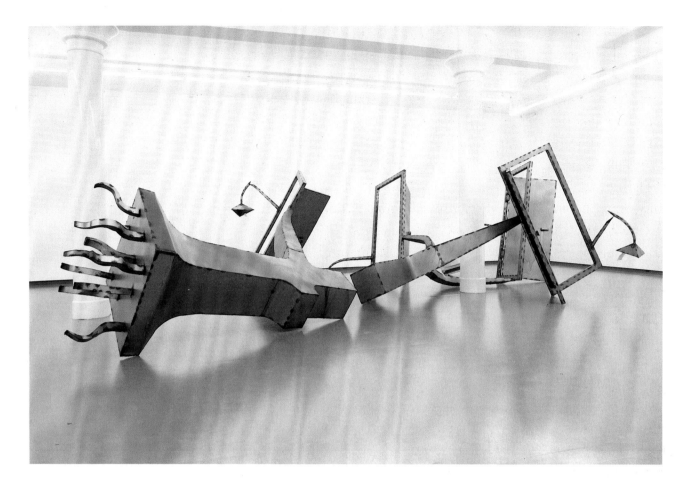

The Last Fruit (The Tree of Idleness) 1988
Steel, television, gold leaf, varnish
222 × 820 × 690cm
Non-extant
BW281

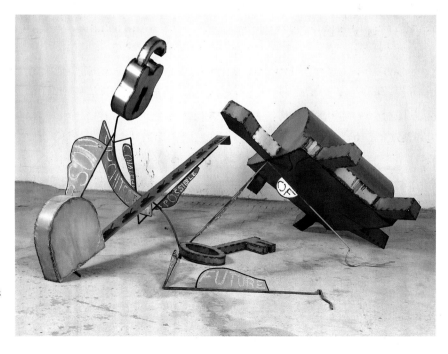

Future Perfect 1988
Steel, varnish
180 × 280 × 320cm
BW300

For Queen and Country 1989
Bronze, gold leaf, enamel paint
121 × 142 × 168cm
BW310

ciations of the craft object might open up new and uncomfortable forms of displacement for sculpture after Post-minimalism and Postmodernism. This is why the overriding character of 'In Awe of the Pawnbroker'(1994) is of scaled-up jewellery and of the gift shop. In this sculpture the gold halos of the 'Little Saints' assume an ostentatious and almost grandiose role, acting not merely as an addendum or exclamation mark but as a structural support. Woodrow cast five large bronze rings set in tassled bronze cushions. On the flattened surface of each ring is a bronze tableau borrowing many of the symbols (pods, coins, spoons, cups) from the earlier work. What connects each tableau, though, is the use of the pawnbroker orbs. In each section of the work they are subject to different scaling and forms of manip-

opposite
Little Saints nos 1–12 1991
Bronze, gold leaf
Nos.1, 4–6 and 9–12: *Private Collections*
BW352–363

Little Saint no.1 23 × 46 × 27cm

Little Saint no.5 21 × 35 × 17cm

Little Saint no.9 36 × 33 × 28cm

Little Saint no.2 23 × 20 × 13cm

Little Saint no.6 21 × 54 × 22cm

Little Saint no.10 33 × 52 × 29cm

Little Saint no.3 27 × 31 × 24cm

Little Saint no.7 5 × 22 × 8cm

Little Saint no.11 45 × 45 × 28cm

Little Saint no.4 30 × 32 × 17cm

Little Saint no.8 35 × 38 × 13cm

Little Saint no.12 45 × 29 × 29cm

In Awe of the Pawnbroker 1994
(detail)
Five bronze units, steel chain
and padlocks
Each unit 195 × 71 × 86cm
Overall size variable
1.95 × 12 × 4m
BW 444

ulation. In one section they twist around each other like a vine, in another
they emerge like flowers from a pod, in another they hang stiffly. Arranged
in a diagonal line and affixed to the wall of the gallery by chains, the effect is
of a morbid folly. A narrative of penury (and usury), the signs of everyday
alienation are given an aesthetic uplift at the hands of craft-like good taste[3].
The result mocks the means employed: the (expensive) bronze casting of
simulated wealth (large gold rings) becomes an elaborate play on the cost of
art at the expense of the social costs of the market economy.

This might seem a profligate way of making such a point, but Woodrow
is nothing if not mischievous. In fact the notion of the folly has been a deci-

3 Each of the rings represents part of a
narrative dealing with the business
of pawnbroking. As Woodrow
describes it, 'the first ring in the
sequence shows the pawnbroker
coming to town, the second is the
pawnbroker finding his premises and
setting up his sign; the third reveals
the interior of the ship; the fourth
deals with the sort of conditions and
environment that gave the pawnbroker his raison d'être; the final
ring comments on the fact that the
pawnbroker, despite the supposed
material progress we have made, has
through history been a permanent
feature'. (*In Awe of the Pawnbroker*,
Oriel Gallery, 1994, p.35.)

4 Although the Ship of Fools is said to have its origins in Greek myth (a group of adventurers embarking on a journey of heroic destiny) actual Ships of Fools are said to have existed in the fourteenth century in Europe. These were boats filled with the insane that were forced to wander from one port and principality to another. The symbolic power of this wandering cargo of the mad and malcontent certainly took hold of the imagination at the end of the Middle Ages (for instance, Hieronymous Bosch's 'Ship of Fools'). By the time of Bosch the notion of the Ship of Fools as an external threat had been transformed into a symbol of anxiety that spoke for peasant and lord. The Ship of Fools encapsulated the very 'folly' of humanity itself (its would-be 'aimless wanderings' and 'material pretensions'). This metaphor though is largely marginal as a mythic resource in Western culture by the beginning of the nineteenth century. The institutionalisation of the insane and the accurate mapping of the earth's waters reduces the imaginary force of the metaphor. Woodrow's use of the image of the Ship of Fools, then, inherits this generalised notion of folly. This is very different from the notion of the *aesthetic* folly which Woodrow employs in all periods of his work, the idea of the work of art as a kind of facetious or dissonant undermining of aesthetic protocol.

sive source of metaphor in his work since the early 1980s. On some occasions he has actually been explicit about this (for instance his adaptation of the medieval tale of the 'Ship of Fools'[4]). Generally, however, the concept has operated as the undisclosed ground of his engagement with the problems and contradictions of modern artistic practice itself. The folly, in these terms, is that set of hoops, traps, stratagems and deviations through which modern artists have to put themselves if they are to continue to defend their autonomy. Thus, the concept of the folly may have its origins in the eighteenth century, but nevertheless there is a sense in which Woodrow's pursuit of the illicit and anomalous is a variant of its demotic, Romantic ideals: to bring the honour and power of official definitions of art into disrepute. This is why Woodrow has also been so keen recently to incorporate the 'fallen' traditions of popular public sculpture and commemoration into his displaced 'world of bronze'. That which has the status of an aesthetic folly for modernist sensibility – the sentimental or populist bronze sculpture – is appropriated and transformed by Woodrow in order to double-code the idea of bronze casting as a critical 'folly'. This is particularly evident in one of Woodrow's most ambitious bronzes, the cannon on loan to the Hat Hill Sculpture Foundation at Goodwood, entitled 'Endeavour (Cannon Dredged from the First Wreck of the "Ship of Fools")' (1990). This represents a life-size ship's cannon, supported by four skeletal animal legs and mounted on an open prison door attached to four wheels. At the front of the base is a

Endeavour (Cannon Dredged from the First Wreck of the 'Ship of Fools') 1990/94
Bronze
205 × 190 × 450cm
Sculpture at Goodwood on loan from the artist
BW328

lupine head whose form mutates at the back into a human foot. This figure is playing an accordian. Next to the cannon is a pile of cannon balls. The work obviously borrows from a tradition of patriotic nautical sculpture, the memorial spiked cannons that are familiar from any number of coastal towns with naval connections. But as in the Imperial War Museum pieces and the 'Little Saints', the comfortable expectations of what bronze casting should do and look like are disordered. In this instance, however, the hybridisation and mutation of form (of the animal into the human, the bodily trapped inside the inanimate) is subject to a greater complexity and wealth of strange detail. This is a monstrous folly, something that, as the title suggests has been dredged up from a place where mutant forms proliferate. Yet this monstrousness is initially deceptive; the mutations and strange details reveal themselves slowly. And this points, particularly in this work, to an increasing reliance in Woodrow's work on the idea of sculpture revealing its meaning through a non-sequential reading of a set of internal symbolic arrangements. This obviously is not only very different from how we read the early work (compare 'Endeavour' to 'Twin-Tub and Guitar') but adapts the idea of montage in sculpture to discernably different ends than previously. The emphasis on the hybridisation of form and the greater stress on the internal symbolic relations between each object pushes Woodrow's 'constellational' approach to montage into a self-enclosed allegorical space, invoking the traditional understanding of allegory as a space in which different moralities compete. The 'Endeavour', for all its ironic repositioning of the low genre of the public memorial, is indebted to the representational space of pre-modern allegorical religious art as a theatre of conflict. Obviously, very different kinds of social experience are being represented in conflict here, yet the idea of 'story-telling' through a 'constellation' of conflicting symbols cannot disguise the pre-modern origins of the work. The monsters invoked here are not those of the temp-tations of the flesh as found in pre-modern allegory, but of the disgorgings of late capitalism. The loss of reason is not invoked through a loss of bodily control but through the failure of capitalism to establish a rational and stable relationship between humans and nature. Furthermore, in the matter of reading, the sculpture pays homage to the serendipities of traditional wood carving and furniture-making, the use of the secret detail to make the owner or user of an object aware of its individual crafting – for instance, the vogue in the nineteenth century for concealed mice and other small creatures on tables or chairs. It is not over-stretching the point to note that the details on the cannon's wheels provide a similar kind of surprise: each wheel doubles as another object (a breadboard, a drum, a role of rope, a support for books) from which protrude other objects signifying various human pleasures.

Where does this all leave Woodrow in relation to his own immediate past? To note these connections between bronze casting and the idea of the 'aesthetic folly', montage and traditional notions of allegory is to see Woodrow steer his commitment to picture-making in sculpture into a space increasingly distant from the agendas of Post-minimalism. By turning to bronze as a disruption of critical Postmodernism's 'business as usual', Woodrow ups the stakes on the role of the artist as 'story-teller' within modern sculpture. Ironically, though, this actually moves him closer to the protocols of Modernism. For, in producing bronze works as integrated sculptural units, the disruptive function of the found object or image is removed. For Modernist abstraction the absence of reference to the world of the everyday object ensured that the art object would remain self-sufficient. The inclusion of the found-object or photograph could only, it was claimed, destroy the integral 'presence' of the work. This is why Woodrow's early sculpture not only owes an extensive debt to Duchamp but also to the extension of Duchamp's legacy in the reaction against Modernist abstraction in American art of the late 1960s. Rauschenberg, Johns and Warhol all based their critique of Modernism on the inclusion of references to everyday life into the symbolically undifferentiated spaces of abstraction (photojournalist imagery in Rauschenberg and Warhol, everyday consumer objects in Johns). Woodrow inherited this dialectic, as does much other contemporary practice which sees the use of such references as a 'direct' route through to the experiences of the everyday. The question, therefore, is, how much does Woodrow see his work now as a critique of this legacy?

In the new sculpture he has clearly sought to produce a formally integrated aesthetic. But this, I would argue, is not to say Woodrow intends to defend conservative notions of presence. On the contrary, in moving into bronze casting, in order to affirm what he sees as the crisis of appropriationist Postmodernism (its actual fetishisation of appropriation), he has had to sacrifice the disruptive logic of the presentation of the found object as a means of making his views on this crisis appear strong and purposeful. In this respect the playful and ironic reworking of bronze casting and its popular genres should be seen as the testing of the academic limits of the permissible and not the substitution of one tradition for another. This means that however we want to describe Woodrow's risk-taking, its outcomes cannot be predicted. Just as Woodrow was never simply a cutter-out of objects, he is not simply a sculptor of bronzes. He is an artist moving in the spaces between traditions and their procedures, in order to destabilise their current comfortable arrangements and settings.

In order to flesh this out, I want to conclude by returning briefly to the issue of the non-specialist or 'philistine' spectator, which I alluded to at the beginning, insofar as the concept of philistinism is crucial to understanding Woodrow's move against the orthodoxies of appropriationist Postmodernism. By philistinism I do not simply mean the pejorative notion of the uncouth and ignorant spectator – a notion inherited in its modern form from Matthew Arnold – but the sense of the philistine as the voice of the excluded, the voice of what is suppressed or repressed by a given specialist or professional account of what passes for the truth of art. On this score there is actually no empirical content to philistinism, the philistine does not exist in a pure state. Rather, what exists are shifting philistine positions, positions that draw attention to how matters of truth and value in art and aesthetics are always determined by relations of power. The philistine, then, is the voice of the contingent disaffirmation of established views of art and aesthetics. As such it should not be identified with a traditional reactive role (what I have called apostasy) but with a desire to adopt a positional response to the avant-garde. This means that philistinism as the voice of the excluded has to be constructed theoretically in response to dominant and prevailing discourses and practices of art and not out of any fixed notion of what is 'popular' or 'not popular', 'advanced' or 'not advanced'. In this the philistine is the 'parasite' on the body of art and aesthetics and not its disgruntled outsider. Woodrow's work embraces this positional, philistine voice, questioning where the boundaries of aesthetics in sculpture are *assumed* to be today. The effect of the bronzes therefore is untoward. The sculptures do not perform in the way advanced sculpture should perform. They 'fuzz up' normal reception. Whether or not this is mere adventitiousness on Woodrow's part will depend on how others put these sculptures to 'work'. For now, however, their awkwardness is as it should be: the voice of the philistine as the voice that dislodges the settled forms of art's attention and judgement.

Bill Woodrow (right) at work in the A B Fine Art Foundry with Tony Gibas, Leslie Glasgow and Marie Madden

Moneyhead 1995
Stone and bronze
100 × 120 × 160cm
BW463

Listening to History 1995
Bronze
75 × 68 × 79cm
BW457

**Endeavour (Cannon
Dredged from the First
Wreck of the 'Ship of
Fools')** 1990/94
Bronze
205 × 190 × 450cm
*Sculpture at Goodwood
on loan from the artist*
BW328

**Anchor (Dredged from
the First Wreck of the
'Ship of Fools')** 1995
Bronze, gold leaf
172 × 230 × 220cm
BW459

Thread Root I 1994
Bronze
35 × 42 × 28cm
BW453

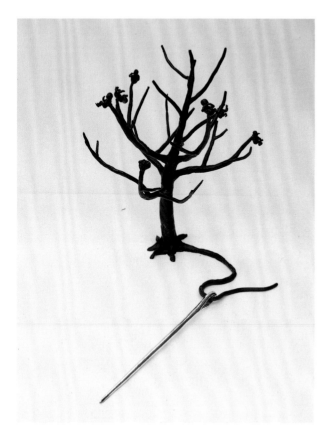

Thread Root II 1994
Bronze
39 × 58 × 35cm
BW454

Thread Root III 1994
Bronze
42.5 × 37 × 26cm
BW455

Sitting on History I 1990/95
Full-size maquette
100 × 107 × 300cm
BW342

Stranger 1990
Bronze, gold leaf
Edition of three
112 × 96 × 72cm
BW341

Orb 1995
Bronze, gold plate, cushion
105 × 67 × 67cm
BW458

Rut 1991
Bronze
Approx. 250 × 400 × 400cm
Kilfane Falls. N. & S. Mosse
BW346

Little Saint no.2 1991
Bronze, gold leaf
23 × 20 × 13cm
BW353

Little Saint no.3 1991
Bronze, gold leaf
27 × 31 × 24cm
BW354

Little Saint no.7 1991
Bronze, gold leaf
5 × 22 × 8cm
BW358

Little Saint no.8 1991
Bronze, gold leaf
35 × 38 × 13cm
BW359

**Self Portrait in the
Year 1990** 1990
Bronze, gold leaf
142 × 205 × 257cm
BW335

Stem 1991
Bronze
152 × 333 × 229cm
BW348

In Awe of the Pawnbroker
1994
Five bronze units, steel chain
and padlocks
Each unit 1.95 × 0.71 × 0.86m
Overall size variable
1.95 × 12 × 4m
Installation: The Model
Arts Centre, Sligo, Ireland,
July 1994
BW444

God Knows 1995
Bronze
740 × 180 × 190cm
BW 467

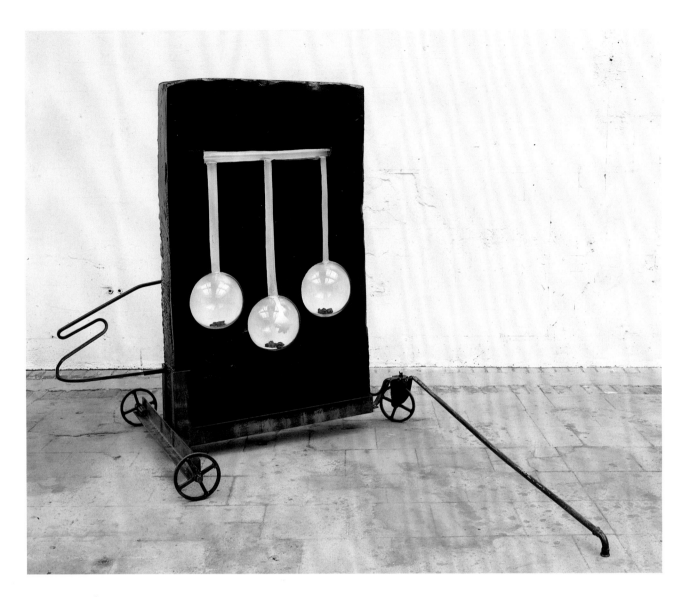

Canary 1992/95
Plaster, steel, glass, coal
154 × 200 × 115cm
BW396

Blade Runner 1995
Bronze
153 × 133 × 118cm
BW461

List of Exhibitions

Bill Woodrow was born in 1948 near Henley, Oxfordshire and now lives and works in London. He trained at Winchester School of Art, Winchester, from 1967–8, Saint Martin's School of Art, London from 1968–71 and Chelsea School of Art, London from 1971–2.

INDIVIDUAL EXHIBITIONS

1972
Whitechapel Art Gallery, London

1979
Kunstlerhaus, Hamburg

1980
The Gallery, Acre Lane, London

1981
L.Y.C. Gallery, Banks, Cumbria
New 57 Gallery, Edinburgh
Galerie Wittenbrink, Regensburg

1982
Lisson Gallery, London
Kunstausstellungen, Stuttgart
Galerie Eric Fabre, Paris
St Paul's Gallery, Leeds
Ray Hughes Gallery, Brisbane
Galerie t'Venster, Rotterdam
Galerie Lachowsky, Antwerp

1983
Galleria Toselli, Milano
Museum van Hedendaagse Kunst, Gent
Lisson Gallery, London
Museum of Modern Art, Oxford
Barbara Gladstone Gallery, New York
Locus Solus, Genoa
art and project, Amsterdam

1984
Mercer Union, Toronto
Musée de Toulon, Toulon
Paul Maenz, Cologne

1985
Kunsthalle Basel, Basel
Barbara Gladstone Gallery, New York
Donald Young Gallery, Chicago
La Jolla Museum of Contemporary Art, La Jolla, California
Currents, ICA, Boston, Massachusetts
Matrix, University Art Museum, University of California, Berkeley

1986
Galerie Nordenhake, Malmo
Paul Maenz, Cologne

Butler Gallery, Kilkenny
Fruitmarket Gallery, Edinburgh
Installation for the Mattress Factory, Pittsburgh

1987
Kunstverein, Munich
Lisson Gallery, London
Cornerhouse, Manchester
Barbara Gladstone Gallery, New York

1988
Paul Maenz, Cologne
Seattle Art Museum, Seattle
Christmas Tree Installation, Tate Gallery, London

1989
Musée des Beaux-Arts, Le Havre, Musée des Beaux-Arts, Calais
Galerie Nordenhake, Stockholm
Mala Galerija, Moderna Galerija, Ljubljana
Fred Hoffman Gallery, Los Angeles
Saatchi Collection, London
Imperial War Museum, London

1990
Galerie Fahnemann, Berlin

1991
XXI São Paulo Bienal, Brazil
Galleria Locus Solus, Genova
Galerie für Druckgrafik, Zürich

1992
Galerie Sabine Wachters, Brussels and Knokke

1993
Quint Krichman Projects, La Jolla, California
Chisenhale Gallery, London and Aspex Gallery, Portsmouth (with Richard Deacon)

1994
Galerie Sabine Wachters, Brussels (with Richard Deacon)
Model Arts Centre, Sligo, Ireland and Limerick City Gallery of Art, Limerick, Ireland
Galerie Sabine Wachters, Brussels and Knokke
Musée Ianchelevici, La Louvière, Belgium

1995
Camden Arts Centre, London and Harris Museum and Art Gallery, Preston

SELECTED GROUP EXHIBITIONS

1981
Objects and Sculpture, Arnolfini, Bristol and ICA, London
British Sculpture in the 20th Century, Whitechapel Art Gallery, London

1982
Biennale of Sydney
Leçons des choses, Kunsthalle, Bern, Musée d'Art et d'Histoire, Chambery, Maison de la Culture, Chalon-sur-Saône, France
Aperto 82, Biennale Di Venezia, Venice
Englische Plastik Heute, Kunstmuseum, Lucerne, Switzerland

1983
Tema Celeste, Museo Civico d'Arte Contemporanea, Gibellina, Italy
Figures and Objects, John Hansard Gallery, Southampton
The Sculpture Show, Hayward Gallery and Serpentine Gallery, London
New Art at the Tate Gallery, Tate Gallery, London
Transformations, XVIII, São Paulo Bienal, Museu de Arte Moderna, Rio de Janiero, Museo de Arte Moderno, Mexico City, Fundação Calouste Gulbenkian, Lisbon

1984
Salvaged, P.S. 1, New York
An International Survey of Recent Painting and Sculpture, Museum of Modern Art, New York
Skulptur Im 20. Jahrhundert, Merian Park, Basel, Switzerland
ROSC '84, The Guinness Hop Store, Dublin, Ireland
The British Art Show, City Museum and Art Gallery, Ikon Gallery, Birmingham, Royal Scottish Academy, Edinburgh, Mappin Art Gallery, Sheffield, Southampton Art Gallery
Deux Regions en France: L'Art international d'aujourd 'hui, Palais des Beaux Arts, Charleroi, Belgium
Images of War, Chapter, Cardiff
The British Show, Art Gallery of Western Australia, Perth, Art Gallery of New South Wales, Sydney, Queensland Art Gallery, Brisbane, Royal Exhibition Building, Melbourne, National Gallery of Art, Wellington, New Zealand
Nouvelle Biennale de Paris '85, Parc de la Villette, Paris
1985 Carnegie International, Museum of Art, Pittsburgh

Select Bibliography

1986

Entre el Objeto y la Imagen, Palacio de Velazquez, Madrid, Centre Cultural de la Caixa de Pensions, Barcelona, Bilbao

Sculpture, 9 Artists from Britain, Louisiana Museum, Humlebaek, Denmark

The Turner Prize, Tate Gallery, London

1987

British Sculpture Since 1965, Museum of Contemporary Art, Chicago and Peace Museum, Chicago, San Francisco Museum of Modern Art, Newport Harbour Art Museum, Hirshhorn Museum, Washington, Albright-Knox Art Gallery, Buffalo

Current Affairs, Museum of Modern Art, Oxford, Mucsarnok, Budapest, Narodni Galerie, Prague, Zacheta, Warsaw

Documenta 8, Kassel, West Germany

1988

Starlit Waters, Tate Gallery, Liverpool

1990

Glasgow's Great British Art Exhibition, McLellan Galleries, Glasgow

1992

BBC Billboard Art Project [In conjunction with Mills and Allen]

1993

Declarations of War, Contemporary Art from the Imperial War Museum, Kettle's Yard Gallery, Cambridge

Recent British Sculpture, Derby Museum and Art Gallery then touring Britain

1994

Sculpture at Goodwood, The Hat Hill Sculpture Foundation, Goodward, West Sussex

A Changing World: 50 Years of Sculpture from the British Council Collection, State Russian Museum, St. Petersburg, Russia

Terrae Motus Terrae Motus, Palazzo Reale, Caserta, Italy

1995

Contemporary British Art in Print, Scottish National Gallery of Modern Art, Edinburgh, 1996 Yale Center for British Art, New Haven, Connecticut

From Picasso to Woodrow: Recently Acquired Prints and Portfolios, Tate Gallery, London

Weltkunst Collection, Irish Museum of Modern Art, Dublin, Ireland

Ripple Across the Water, Watari-Um, The Watari Museum of Contemporary Art, Tokyo, Japan

Soyons Serieux ..., Musée d'art moderne, Villeneuve d'Ascq, France

Bill Woodrow, Galerie Wittenbrink, Regensburg 1981.

Beaver, Bomb and Fossil, Museum of Modern Art, Oxford 1983. Text by David Elliott.

Bill Woodrow, Kunsthalle, Basel 1985. Text by Jean-Christophe Amman.

Natural Produce, an Armed Response. Sculpture by Bill Woodrow, La Jolla Museum of Contemporary Art, California 1985. Texts by Hugh M. Davies and Lynda Forscha.

Bill Woodrow. Sculpture 1980–86, Fruitmarket Gallery, Edinburgh 1986. Text by Lynne Cooke.

Bill Woodrow, Kunstverein München, Munich 1987. Text by Lynne Cooke.

Bill Woodrow. Eye of the Needle, Musée des Beaux-Arts, Le Havre 1989. Texts by Catherine Grenier and Françoise Cohen.

Bill Woodrow. Point of Entry. New Sculptures. Selima Hill. Poems Written in Response to the Sculptures, Imperial War Museum, London 1989.

Bill Woodrow, Moderna Galerija, Ljubljana 1989. Text by Françoise Cohen.

Bill Woodrow. XXI Bienal de São Paolo 1991, British Council, London 1991. Text by John Roberts.

Only the Lonely and Other Shared Sculptures: Bill Woodrow and Richard Deacon, Chisenhale Gallery, London 1993. Text by Bill Woodrow and Richard Deacon.

Chapter and Verse, Maison de la Culture, La Louviere, Belgium 1994. Interview with Eddy Devolder.

In Awe of the Pawnbroker, Oriel, Cardiff 1995. Text by John Roberts.

Bill Woodrow: About this Axis. Drawings 1990–95, Camden Arts Centre, London 1995.

Index of Exhibited Works

All works belong to the artist
unless otherwise stated.

**Anchor (Dredged from the First
Wreck of the 'Ship of Fools')** 1995
Bronze, gold leaf
172 × 230 × 220cm
BW459
Illustrated on p.37

Blade Runner 1995
Bronze
153 × 133 × 118cm
BW461
Illustrated on p.53

Canary 1992/95
Plaster, steel, glass and coal
154 × 200 × 115cm
BW396
Illustrated on p.52

**Endeavour (Cannon Dredged
from the First Wreck of the
'Ship of Fools')** 1990/94
Bronze
205 × 190 × 450cm
*Sculpture at Goodwood on loan
from the artist*
BW328
Illustrated on p.36

God Knows 1995
Bronze
740 × 180 × 190cm
BW467
Illustrated on p.51

In Awe of the Pawnbroker 1994
Five bronze units, steel chain
and padlocks
Each unit 1.95 × 0.71 × 0.86m
Overall size variable 1.95 × 12 × 4m
BW444
Illustrated on pp.48–9

Listening to History 1995
Bronze
75 × 68 × 79cm
BW457
Illustrated on p.35

Little Saint no.2 1991
Bronze, gold leaf
23 × 20 × 13cm
BW353
Illustrated on p.44

Little Saint no.3 1991
Bronze, gold leaf
27 × 31 × 24cm
BW354
Illustrated on p.44

Little Saint no.7 1991
Bronze, gold leaf
5 × 22 × 8cm
BW358
Illustrated on p.45

Little Saint no.8 1991
Bronze, gold leaf
35 × 38 × 13cm
BW359
Illustrated on p.45

Moneyhead 1995
Stone and bronze
100 × 120 × 160cm
BW463
Illustrated on p.34

Orb 1995
Bronze, gold plate, cushion
105 × 67 × 67cm
BW458
Illustrated on p.42

Rut 1991
Bronze
Approx. 250 × 400 × 400cm
Kilfane Falls. N. & S. Mosse
BW346
Illustrated on p.43

Self Portrait in the Year 1990 1990
Bronze, gold leaf
142 × 205 × 257cm
BW335
Illustrated on p.46

Sitting on History I 1990/95
Bronze
100 × 107 × 300cm
BW342
Maquette illustrated on p.40

Stem 1991
Bronze
152 × 333 × 229cm
BW348
Illustrated on p.47

Stranger 1990
Bronze, gold leaf
Edition of three
112 × 96 × 72cm
BW341
Illustrated on p.41

Thread Root I 1994
Bronze
35 × 42 × 28cm
BW453
Illustrated on p.38

Thread Root II 1994
Bronze
39 × 58 × 35cm
BW454
Illustrated on p.39

Thread Root III 1994
Bronze
42.5 × 37 × 26cm
BW455
Illustrated on p.39